BLUES

POEMS N' SUCH

SUKRITI KIRAN

This book would not be possible without the support of my family - my mother who

has supported me through thick and thin . My chosen family of my friends - Abhilasha, Nikita, Sugandha ,

Anuja , Astha, Akshita and Aishani.

Also, want to thank my middle school literature teacher Preeti mam.(I still seek your validation.)

My sincere apologies if I forgot anyone to mention here.

Contents

Preface

Hello, i'm Sukriti and this is my best (perhaps not the best) attempt at writing some poems .

I chose this medium to express my feelings and also to share with the world because i truly believe that no

matter who you are, where you are from, you can always find people who want to be with you and relate to you .

You can always find your Tribe .

Acknowledgements

A special thanks to Aishani for her constant encouragement to pursue my creative endeavours.

Daydreaming

been dreaming about us

you and me

cuddling and kissing

holding our faces

it comes with an afterthought

it comes with a lump in the throat

you aren't here

nor you will be

been daydreaming all this while

because i have nothing to go on

your presence gave me hope

but i am not the wings

i am the rope

can't be alright,

this can't be alright

it was always out of might

i wouldn't leave ,

nor would you

been daydreaming all this while

because i had nothing to go on

hope comes with a price

it takes up a slice

of your solace

and carves out a place

that place then feels empty

makes you hungry and thirsty

makes you want to fill it up with poison

and there can't be enough reason

its antidote is not yet discovererd

and what is lost

can’t be recovered

we have got to hold on

for our other dreams are forlorn .

Boxes

put it in a box

label it ASAP

tie it up

so it won't snap

boxes we have of emotions

love and grief goes in ones

boxes we have of anger

labelled as right or wrongs

boxes we have of lust

mine is filled with dust

boxes we have in the attic

we put them away to be pragmatic

boxes we have unlabelled

because we don't understand

boxes we receieved

some we created ourselves to be there

but we won't talk about it here

boxes we have from unrequited Love

because we didin't know where to shove

boxes we have from parents

which we inherit through generations

boxes we have for ourselves

which go empty , as we peek in

these should be filled beforehand

before we donate ourselves to somebody's Hand

these are the important ones

which we don't know about

we just keep giving out

emptiness inside this box

must be filled up

only then we're ready to receive Love

Sad songs

i opened up my soul

and i poured out a glass full

although it was appetizing

it smelled quite foul

I soasked it on the paper

and it was torn

I arranged it in some sorts

and it became a sad song

pain was shadowed by the aesthetics

and issues became theatrics

my heart reached out for someone's hand

but it became a sad song

my grief became the plot

and my love became the tragedy

although no one united in the end

but somehow it is a comedy

my protagonist hasn't change a a bit

my hero is still a child

the circumstances have emerged victorious

and she has lost her mind .

Witch house

i visited the old house

nothing of value remained

i returnded to the old bedroom

it lay opened

i touched the memories

they came alive crying

whispering and moanng

the good ol'stories

i moved to the kitchen

where potions lay bubbling

i stayed there for longer

where magic was brewing

i tasted a spoonful

and my heart became full

it filled with emptiness

and it filled with spells

spells of what it could have been

spells of what it has been

my face turned old

my heart shrank

i saw myself grow

i saw myself go blank

i crept into a corner

and became a memory

i hung on a wall

and became a story .

Like falling in a dream

Running with your legs tied

walking on the moving ground

swimming upside down

alive but mummified

when you fall in a dream

why does it feel real

does it invoke muscle memories

has it happened before ?

remembering mental rashes

waking up with flashes

real or fiction ?

have you noticed we wake up before -

-before, we'd have crashed

leaving us ashore

what would it feel like to finally

meet the ground

crashing in finally

how good does it sound?

Happy place

what is this happy place people talk about

i have never even had one -

-one place, i mean,

why is the place so happy about?

this place has been empty

disheveled and cabinets open

as if looted and abandoned

but that is where i live

that place is just a place

that place is nothing more to me

no fun times in the past

no memories, no story

whether it was concrete

or just a person,

felt like the same

whether it was moving or or fixed

it felt like a dream

never found a permanent

home and ,or, people

never thought there will be

a chosen family or should i steal ?

i have been calling fleeting memories my life

been calling passing people my own

i feel like i am standing

and life is passing me by like a ghost

Bittersweet

my dreams and yours cannot unite

and praying has not helped

losing my religion, and

been struggling for respite

staying or leaving

can not decide

hoping for the impossible

can’t open my eyes

happy for you, truly i am

but i'm sad for myself too

its all so bittersweet

its all so bittersweet

your arguments make more sense

and my whimpers don’t

all are stick and stones,

love is skin and bones

i have accepted it since

loving you makes no sense

but i can't stop it

but i can't stop it

highs and lows are stuck together

ups and downs are forever

why can't we be like that

why can't we be like that

when will the ends meet

been waiting for a purer scent

no highs no lows , just constant

its all so bittersweet

its all so bittersweet

Hummingbird

little birdie out it in the Vast

looking for the sweet nectar

roaming from flower to flower

very much like my heart

she loves the sweetness

she loves the fast heat

she love the quivering heartbeat

she can disapeear in the vastness-

-vastness , is what is scary

different places and

she is so tiny

how will she live

how will she survive

how will she find

the love of her life

why can't there be less adventures

why can't there be more calm

but people raised in a hurricane

call storms as their home .

Earthquake

shaking and cracking my life open

shriveling lungs and organs

pouring out the blood from the pipes

tsunamis and releasing the Kraken

letting the lava pour out

letting my world come down

i released all the anguish

i released the hell from beneath

no more facade of sanity

no more drapes of civilization

we take the world as it is

no more past life's dignity

uprooting the trees of relation

upwelling of the oceans -

-oceans of anger and frustration

i seek no redemption

i just seek justice

i have no desire else

than just vengeance

i want the world to crumble

just like mine

i want all of them out

just like mine .

Grief

how does one deal with grief

how does one cut love at brief

how can you stop loving someone

i have asked myself

and i have asked eveyone

all of them gave the same answer-

-answer, that made no sense

love dies but leaves its essence

how can somone put it somewhere

how can someone know exactly where ?

it goes away after a while

it is felt less after sometime

it does not go away , no it does not

it just grows old and senile

it wouldn't remember who you were

it would forget your face

it wouldn't recognise the touch

but it is still there.

Uncertainty

i was hoping and thinking

about the stuff what will be

you can run all you want

but things are meant to be

yet this uncertainty remains

filling up the palms of my hands

yet this uncertainty remains

filling up with sands

castles of hope, building and eroding

going up and down

right and left, sliding

highs of highs and lows of lows

after an epoch

it becomes numb

you can stomach

more than you can think

we grow older

in the name of strength

we go dumber

in the name of wisdom

it has aged on me now

i have learned to be better

it has broken me now

and i am not bitter

mending and trying the pieces on

growing in the broken pots

things fade even the ones

etched on stone

filling up the heart with hope

filling up the palms with hope

trust me, i'm trying to be better

as broken crayons still colour .

Name a hero who was happy

the way it goes

the beating, the falling

the kicking, the waiting

the violence it took

to become this gentle

the menace it took

to become this normal

the scars left behind

leaves us with guilt

the stories that are etched

sometimes they split-

-split the souls in pieces

so we can recollect them

examining everything and

weighing in scales

the constant scrutiny it takes

it leaves no validation

the mess it makes of us

it leaves out no salvation

the origins were harsh

so we chose a different path

that drove us apart

from what we were

the punches , the fists

hardly people know

that heroes don't exist

it's just people, struggling

trying and trying .

Poison

colours were alive

hallucinating all over

taking over the world

poison in the blood

getting the flights

going the heights

falling the lows

facing the blows

life flashes in eight by ten

posion takes over again

eyes go black and blue

and pain,though it remains true-

-true to me and nobody else

nobody comes into the safe place

you are unwelcome in your home

one mistake and its etched on stone

the more superior form is of course, the Pain

grief, love , attachment -

comes in shapes and names

my love has turned in grief

like heat turns in to rains .

Roses and thorns

Should Roses be coupled with Pricks ?

what does it say about the Beauty

some risks added to someone beautiful

should it be paired with Beasts ?

something so soft and troubled forever-

-forever will be picked

hence the added danger

consequences of picking the flower

must be in place

or it will not bloom perhaps

surrounded with fear

lovers waiting for the spring

so are the gardeners

as the vanity it will bring

roses wincing in pain

and thorns can't do much

new beginnings happened

from the thorn's bottom

still the blossom

is the one that is the loved .

Untouchable

i don't understand

what had just happened

for what was worth

it did unearth

some tragic fire

but it cooled and solidified

around my charred heart

it was so close

still i could not touch it

it was so dear

still i could not smooch it

my heart tried

but couldnt bleed

so we tried

but could not succeed

you were in my hands

but not in my fate

we always had to wait

i could not wrap my head around it

i could not be proud of it

why did it happen

that is what i ask

why did it have

a love full of sparks

i don't understand

what had just happened .

Red, Blue and Green

"Red" stains everything

existing becomes living

the first Hallows-

everything soft and exciting

what they do ,what they say

we observe and follow

smiling and giddy all the time

high as high one can go

free and galloping with joy

then comes the "Blue"part

everything coloured with sorrow

lovesickness cures and comes the new issues

you said this and you did that

it won't kill us to be apart

then the "Green" arrives

if somewhow we survived

it turns into envy

the solace it brings with hate

all the things of privy

colours change as we go

that is how it is meant to be

but people are mess of different things

everyone, you and me

things don't last

even if we stayed apart

won't we see the same colours ?

broken colours will still stain

bleeding away when soaked again .

Overold

wrinkles and lines

beers and wines

sticks and meds

diapers and aids

it bleeds, it hurts

it needs some help

it needs to get some support

to get back on its own

its slow and irregular

its chaos and thunder

its lazy and shriveled

it is awful and smelly

it has a shrunk belly

it has less fire left in it

it has more stories to tell

it has mourned and moved on

it has grieved and stayed on

it has nothing to do with the body

as it hasn't grown old

it is the heart that is weary

and it has grown Overold

Write one of your own poems <3

Printed by Libri Plureos GmbH in Hamburg, Germany